Great-great-
Grandpa's
travel gear

CAMERA
EQUIPMENT

Phoebe and Felix
Fogg are exploring their
attic one rainy day, when they stumble
on some boxes that used to belong to their great-great-
grandpa, Phileas Fogg. It turns out that he was a famous explorer, who
went around the whole world in 80 days! They spend hours reading all about his
incredible adventures in dozens of fascinating countries. Then, they have an idea!
They want to follow in their ancestor's footsteps and set out on their own epic
journey around the world, with their pet parrot and best friend Passepartout …
and they want you to come with them!

So, pack your suitcase, grab your passport, and get ready to join Phoebe, Felix,
and Passepartout on the most exciting adventure of your life, discovering new
things and solving some clever activities along the way!

CONTENTS

Use this page to track Felix, Phoebe, and Passepartout's journey around the globe!

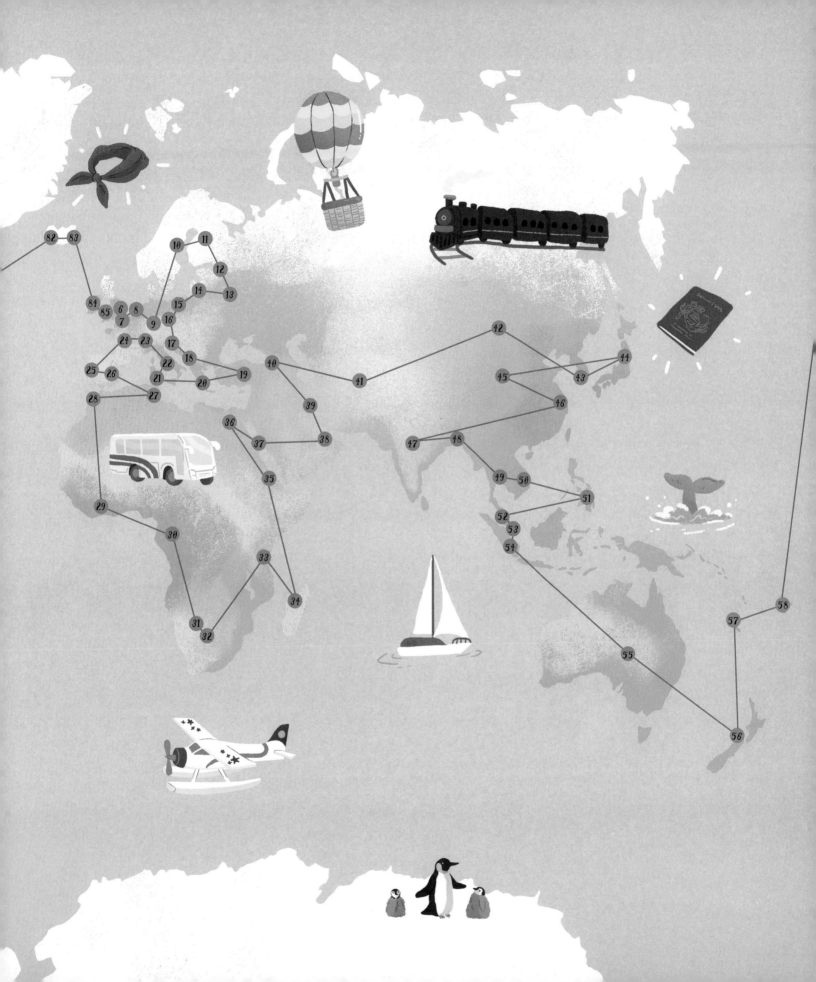

ODD RAVEN OUT

Before they depart on their epic voyage, the children and Passepartout visit the Tower of London in the UK. There, they meet a guard, who is feeding the ravens. Can you spot a raven that is not like the others?

England, UK

RUN FOR THE BUS!

The kids need to catch the bus to the airport in London to get started on their journey. Use the clues to find the right bus for them:

Their bus route's number is not a prime number.

Their driver is not wearing a hat.

Their driver is holding the steering wheel.

Their bus route's number is not a multiple of 7.

9

258

105

114

23

MADE IN EDAM

Soon the children arrive in the Netherlands. They visit the famous cheese market in the town of Edam. Can you spot eight differences between these selfies?

The Netherlands

BIRD'S-EYE VIEW

Phoebe and Felix have gone to Neuschwanstein Castle in Germany for the day, but they can't find Passepartout. Can you spot him making friends with the castle residents? How many other birds are there in this picture?

SWEDISH MIDSUMMER MATCH

Using the pieces at the bottom of the page, complete this jigsaw puzzle of the Foggs' trip to the midsummer festival in Sammilsdal, Sweden. Which one doesn't belong?

A B C D E

Sweden

FAIRYTALE FOREST

The Foggs are on a wildlife-spotting trek in a fairytale forest in Finland. Phoebe is looking for lily of the valley flowers, and Felix is seeking brimstone butterflies. Count how many there are of each. Are there more of Phoebe's flowers or Felix's butterflies in this glade?

TAXI TARIFF

The children are taking a taxi ride at 7 a.m. across St. Petersburg, Russia. Using the price list below, can you work out how much their fare will come to? They have two bags and a pet (Passepartout), and their journey is 10 km (6.2 miles) long. How much would the same journey cost at 10 p.m.?

Taxi start fare: 100 rubles

Each bag: 10 rubles

Each pet: 25 rubles

Each 1 km (0.62 mile): 20 rubles

Extra charge of 20 percent for journeys between 8 p.m. and 6 a.m.

BOLSHOI BALLET

Felix and Phoebe are watching the famous Bolshoi Ballet in Moscow, Russia. Which silhouette is the only one that exactly matches the scene on stage?

A   B   C   D

LITHUANIAN LUNCH

Felix and Phoebe are ordering lunch at a restaurant in Vilnius, Lithuania. Passepartout can't wait and has been given a banana for free! They both decide to have the borscht soup to start with, then Felix chooses the dumplings and Phoebe goes for the kugelis. They will share a slice of blueberry pie for dessert. Felix wants an apple juice and Phoebe wants a hot chocolate. What will the total bill add up to?

Borscht

MENU

Kugelis

APPETIZERS AND MAINS
Borscht €2.75
Chicken soup €3.25
Traditional dumplings €5.00
Sandwiches €4.50
Kugelis €4.20

DESSERTS
Ice cream €1.75
Pie of the day €3.20

DRINKS
Cola €1.75
Fruit juices €2.00
Hot chocolate €2.75

Blueberry pie

GNOME WAY OUT

The Foggs are visiting a busy market square in Wrocław, Poland. How many traditional gnomes are there hidden in this scene?

STATUE STILL

Prague in the Czech Republic is famous for its many statues—Charles Bridge alone has 30! Carefully copy this statue of the renowned knight Bruncvík, using the grid to help you.

Czech Republic

SLOVENIAN STYLE

The Fogg children are enjoying a craft afternoon, learning how to paint traditional Slovenian decorated eggs. Create your own designs in the blank eggs.

PELICAN PUZZLER

Felix and Phoebe are counting pelicans in Croatia.
Can you spot which of these Dalmatian pelicans is
slightly different from the others?

B

A

D

C

E

OUTFIT ADDITION

The Foggs left their baggage on the train from Croatia to Turkey, so they need to buy an outfit each to wear until their baggage arrives. They have a total of 1,000 lira to spend in this Turkish market.

Can you work out how much it will cost if they each buy one set of underwear, socks, a T-shirt, and some shorts? Will they have enough left over to buy an ice cream each? Ice creams cost 50 lira each.

175 LIRA

125 LIRA

50 LIRA
per pair

70 LIRA

ACROPOLIS ACTION

The children and Passepartout are visiting the Acropolis in Athens, Greece. They have arranged to meet with a tour guide at one of the statues but there's one problem … they don't know which statue! Use the following clues to find the right statue:

The statue doesn't have a head.

The statue is not holding a weapon.

The statue is wearing a necklace.

Only one of the statue's hands is visible.

One foot is raised off the ground.

A

B

C

D

E

F

G

H

BEACH VISIT

Can you join the dots to reveal the very special visitor the Foggs saw on the beach as they windsurfed in the Mediterranean Sea?

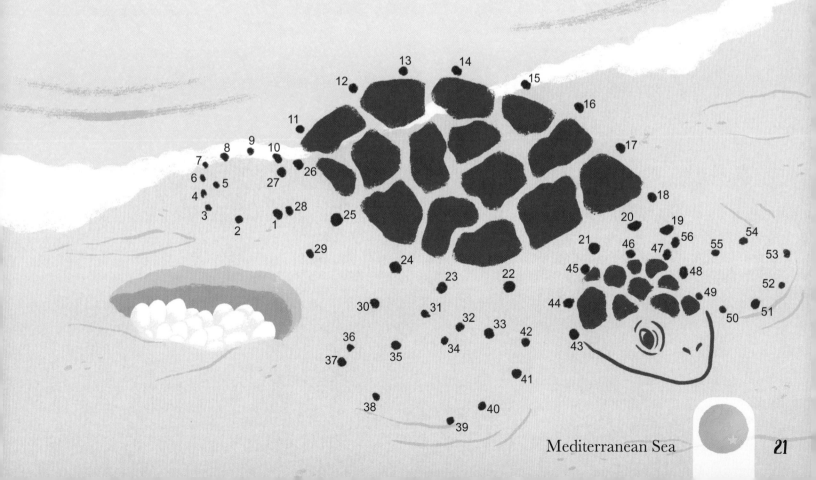

OLIVE HARVEST

Can you spot 10 differences between these pictures of the Fogg children collecting olives in Liguria, Italy?

Italy

SUMMER IN SWITZERLAND

The children are having a picnic. How many alpine marmots can you spot hidden in this meadow in Switzerland?

PÂTISSERIE PIECES

The children are choosing a cake or pastry from a pâtisserie in Paris, France. Complete this scene using the pieces below, then work out which one doesn't belong in the picture.

A B C D E F

France

TILE DESIGN

Portugal is famous for its beautiful tiles. Design your own tiles here. The first two have been done for you, as examples that you can shade in.

Shade in all the boxes that contain the letters S, P, A, I, or N. The remaining letters spell the name of the Spanish city the Foggs are visiting.

P	S	T	I	A
S	A	S	I	O
P	L	N	A	S
S	N	E	N	S
A	I	S	N	I
N	A	I	P	D
I	O	P	N	A
P	S	A	S	I

TUNISIAN TONES

The children have bought a traditional carpet in Tunisia. Use your brightest pencils to fill in the pattern with reds, blues, greens, and golds, or whatever shades you prefer.

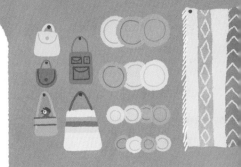

Tunisia

FOSSIL HUNT

The Foggs and Passepartout are fossil hunting in the desert near Erfoud, Morocco. Felix is looking for trilobite fossils, like the one he is holding, and Phoebe is trying to find ammonite fossils, like the one she is pointing at. Who will find the most?

Morocco

HIGH FASHION

The Ébrié people of the Côte'd'Ivoire often wear brilliantly patterned clothes. Can you design some outfits for these two people?

BIRD SPOTTING

The Foggs are spending the day looking for birds in a tropical forest in the Congo. Can you spot these six birds?

SPOTSWANA

Phoebe, Felix, and Passepartout are very lucky and have found one of the world's rarest mammals while on their safari tour in Botswana. Join the dots to see what it is.

DANCE, DANCE

Felix and Phoebe are at a festival in Botswana, watching some Phathisi dancing. Which picture is the odd one out?

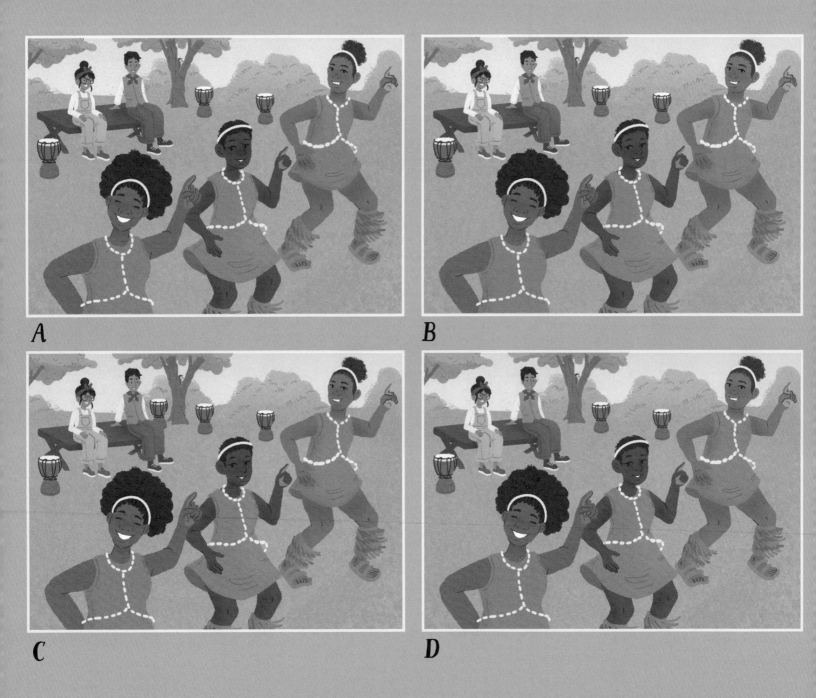

A

B

C

D

BEAD-OKU

Complete this grid using the six Tanzanian beads below. Can you place the beads once in each column, row, and mini grid?

CHAMELEON CAMOUFLAGE

On a walk through the jungle of Madagascar, Phoebe and Felix have spotted a beautiful chameleon. Can you spot six differences between the top and bottom images?

SNACK DROP

The Foggs brought 10 bananas for their trip to the volcanic springs at Dallol in Ethiopia, but they've dropped them accidentally. Can you spot all 10?

TEMPLE PUZZLE

This jigsaw of the Temple of Hatshepsut in Egypt has one too many pieces.
Can you complete the puzzle, then work out which piece doesn't fit?

A

B

C

D

E

F

SCUBA SURPRISE

Cross out all the letters in the name GULF OF AQABA. The remaining letters spell the name of the interesting thing the Foggs have found while diving in the Red Sea.

G S U H L I F P
O W F R A E Q
C A K B A

DESERT DAYS

The Foggs are riding in a dune buggy in the desert in the United Arab Emirates. Which path leads back to their hotel?

C

B

A

United Arab Emirates

SKETCH MATCH

Phoebe has been sketching the skyline of the beautiful city of Yazd, Iran. Which of these drawings exactly matches the skyline?

A

B

C

D

A PICTURE OF PEACE

Phoebe and Felix are visiting Tbilisi in Georgia. Use the grid to help you copy this picture of them on the Bridge of Peace over the Kura River.

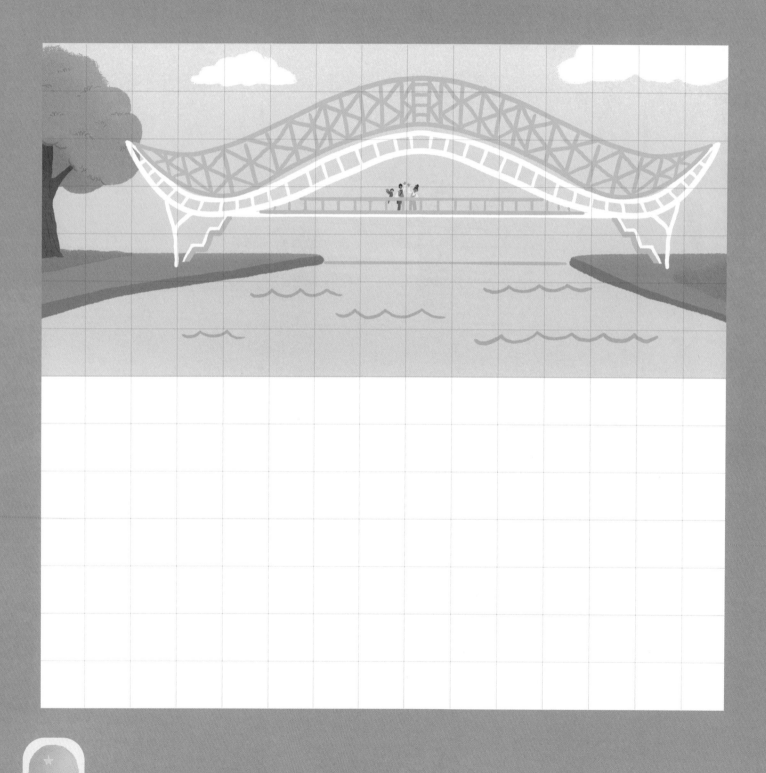

Georgia

HUNT THE CAP

Passepartout has dropped his cap in one of the traditional pots at this stall in Istālif, Afghanistan. Follow the clues to find out which vessel it is in.

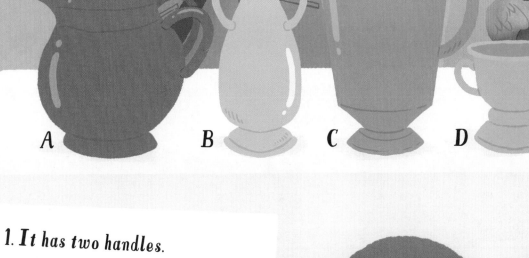

A B C D E

1. It has two handles.
2. It is taller than Passepartout.
3. It does not have a spout.
4. It does not have a fluted top.

IN PLAIN SIGHT

Phoebe and Felix are riding horses in the Mongolian plains to get to their home for the night—a ger (a traditional tent). Put this muddled-up picture in the right order by writing the numbers in the spaces below.

1   2   3   4   5   6   7   8   9   10

__   __   __   __   __   __   __   __   __   __

Mongolia

DINNER IS SERVED

The Foggs are in Seoul, eating South Korea's famous bibimbap —rice served with a combination of meat, vegetables, pickles, and often topped with an egg. Draw the bibimbap you'd most like to eat, with your choice of ingredients.

고추장 GOCHUJANG

KIMONO SHOW

The children have been trying on kimonos, the traditional dress of Japan. Use your pens and pencils to finish this picture of them in their new outfits.

Japan

ODD WARRIOR OUT

Which of these five terracotta warriors in Shaanxi, China, is not the same as the others?

A

B

D

C

E

BOAT TRIP

Cross out all the letters in the word BOAT TRIP. The remaining letters spell the name of the city in China the Foggs are visiting today.

OBATASBHBEA
TПABZOBTHAO
TAEBTПOAB

FANTASTIC FRUIT

See if you can spot 10 differences between these two pictures of the Foggs shopping at a fruit stall in India.

FOREST FAUNA

Felix and Phoebe are spotting wildlife in a forest in Bangladesh. Can you find each of these five animals they're hoping to see?

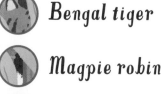 Bengal tiger

 Magpie robin

Gibbon

 Gaur

King cobra

Bangladesh

BEACH PIECES

This jigsaw puzzle of a beautiful beach in Thailand isn't quite finished.
Add the final pieces to complete the picture. Which piece doesn't fit?

MONKEY SPOT

Felix and Phoebe are exploring a tropical forest in northern Vietnam. How many macaque monkeys have joined them for a snack?

COCONUT CONUNDRUM

Cross out all the letters in the word FRESH BUKO. The remaining letters spell the name of the city in the Philippines in which the Foggs are enjoying a refreshing drink of green coconut water, which is called buko by locals.

OMKFUERBA
ESNHSIHRLB
FUAFKROU

TALL TOWERS

The Foggs and Passepartout are vising the famous Petronas Twin Towers in Kuala Lumpur, Malaysia. Join the dots to discover what they look like.

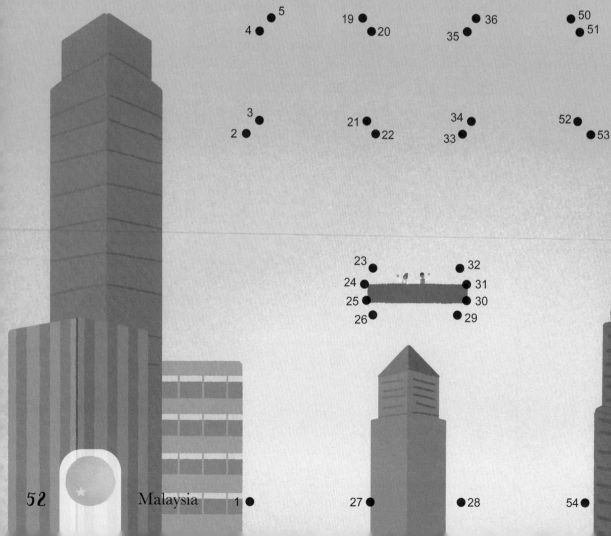

Malaysia

MERLION MATCH

The Merlion is a mythical creature with the body of a fish and the head of a lion, and is the symbol of Singapore. Can you spot which silhouette doesn't match the picture here?

A

B

C

D

BALI CLIFF CLIMB

The Foggs are rock climbing in Bali, Indonesia. Which rope path leads to the top of the cliff?

A

B

C

D

E

F

Indonesia

MAGNIFICENT MONOLITH

The Foggs are enjoying spotting animals in a famous place in Australia. Cross out all the letters in the name ULURU. The remaining letters spell the name of an animal native to Australia.

URWULUOLUML
RRULUBRLRUAU
LRUTLURL

CARVING CLASS

The Foggs are learning how to make Māori carvings in Te Puia, Rotorua, New Zealand. Can you spot eight differences between these scenes?

New Zealand

TURTLE-Y AMAZING

Felix and Phoebe have enjoyed looking at art while they have been in Polynesia. Can you fill in the turtle on the right with some Polynesian-style markings?

SHELL SHORE

The children are exploring a beach in Fiji. Can you spot which of the shells they've been studying doesn't have an exact match?

Fiji

ALASKAN ADVENTURE

Use your pens or pencils to finish this scene of the Foggs' day out kayaking on an Alaskan lake.

Alaska, USA

PLANTDOKU

Complete this grid using the six native plants of western Canada below.
Can you place these plants once each in each column, row, and mini grid?

British Columbia, Canada

CAMP ALBERTA

The Foggs are camping by a lake in Alberta, Canada, but they have misplaced a few items. Can you help Felix find his passport, hat, shoe, and sunglasses, and Phoebe locate her backpack, pen, and sweater?

COWBOY COUNTRY

Phoebe and Felix are on a pony trek in the mountains of Wyoming, USA. Add the pieces to complete the picture. Which one doesn't fit?

A   B   C   D   E

CACTUS COUNT

Are there more rock squirrels or desert cacti in this Texan landscape in the USA?

WAVE RIDER

Join the dots to find out what sport Phoebe is trying in California, USA.

BEAD BRILLIANCE

The Foggs have been learning how to design traditional Huichol beaded bracelets at a craft workshop in Mexico. Fill in the blank bracelets with similar designs.

IT ALL ADDS UP

The Foggs are enjoying a delicious dinner at a cafe in Costa Rica. Passepartout's meal is free, courtesy of the generous cafe owners. How much will it cost in total if Felix has the set menu, a dessert, and an orange juice, and Phoebe has the set menu and a grape juice?

DRINKS
Fresh grape juice ₡100
Fresh orange juice ₡200
Cola ₡150

SET MENU
1 appetizer and 1 main course ₡450

Add a dessert for just ₡200

HATCHING OUT

Can you spot which of these silhouettes exactly matches the picture of these hatchling turtles in the Galápagos Islands?

A

B

C

D

CLIMBING IN COLOMBIA

The Foggs are on a nature-spotting trip in Colombia. How many agile spider monkeys are hiding near this waterfall?

SEEING DOUBLE

Use the grid to help you copy this cute picture of a llama in Peru.

PERU PATTERNS

Join Felix and Phoebe in learning how to design these traditional Peruvian Quechua scarves. Use your brightest pens or pencils to bring the patterns to life.

EASTER SURPRISE

Can you spot which of these ancient Easter Island statues doesn't quite match the others?

A B C D E

HANDS ON

One of these handprints is not like the others at the Cueva de las Manos in Argentina—a cave containing 9,000-year-old handprint decorations. Can you spot the one with five fingers and a thumb?

Argentina

ANTARCTIC CRUISE

Phoebe and Felix have gone on a cruise around the Southern Ocean, where they're on the lookout for penguins. Can you spot six differences in these pictures?

SOUTHERN CROSS

Can you match the missing puzzle pieces to the correct spots in the picture of this peaceful kayaking scene in Antarctica? Which one doesn't belong?

A

B

C

D

E

SNACK BREAK

The children have spilled their snacks on the overnight bus in Argentina and need to collect them all up. Can you find two sandwiches, two bananas, two juice boxes, and two cookies hidden in this scene?

BRAZILIAN FRUIT-DOKU

Complete this grid using the six Brazilian fruits below. Can you place them once each in each column, row, and mini grid?

JUNGLE FEVER

Use your brightest pens or pencils to finish
this brilliant scene of the Amazon jungle
in Brazil.

Brazil

GUESSING IN GUYANA

Connect the dots to find out what animal the Foggs have spotted in Guyana.

Guyana

BEACH BALL

The children are having fun in Barbados. Which of these silhouettes exactly matches the real scene?

A

B

C

D

SOUVENIR HUNTING

The children are shopping in Jamaica. Felix buys two towels, a backpack, and a pair of sandals. Phoebe buys a T-shirt, a ball, a sunhat, and a pair of sunglasses. Who pays the most for all of their items?

$2.50

$5

$1

$6

$7.50

$9

$5

COUNTING CABS

After a busy afternoon in Central Park, Felix and Phoebe are trying to get back to their New York City hotel in the USA. Are there more bicycles or yellow cabs in this busy scene?

CRACK THE CASE

The Foggs are waiting to collect their baggage at the airport in Iceland. Use these clues to help them spot it:

Their baggage has a green ribbon on the handle.

Their baggage has wheels.

Their baggage does not have a fragile sticker.

Their baggage does not have any pockets.

ICE COLD

Phoebe and Felix are trying on traditional lopapeysa sweaters in Iceland.
Can you brighten up the patterns with your best pens or pencils?

THE JIG IS UP

Can you spot the dancer whose outfit doesn't match the others at this Irish dancing show in Dublin, Ireland?

A

B

C

D

E

ALL ABOARD!

Can you spot eight differences between these pictures of the children on the Ffestiniog Railway in the Welsh highlands, before they head back to London?

Solutions

PAGE 6

PAGE 7

The answer is Bus 9.

PAGE 8

PAGE 9

There are 14 other birds.

PAGE 10

The answer is E.

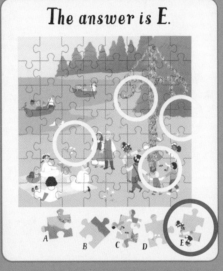

PAGE 11

There are 14 butterflies and 12 flowers, so there are more butterflies.

PAGE 12

The 7 a.m. fare will cost 100 + 10 + 10 + 25 + 200 rubles = 345 rubles.

20 percent of 345 is 69 so the 10 p.m. fare will cost 69 rubles + 345 rubles = 414 rubles.

PAGE 13

The answer is **D**.

PAGE 14

The answer is:

€2.75 + €2.75 + €5.00
+ €4.20 + €3.20 + €2.00
+ €2.75 = €22.65.

PAGE 15

There are seven gnomes.

PAGE 18

The answer is **A**.

PAGE 19

The answer is:
each outfit costs 70 + 50 + 125 + 175 lira = 420 lira. So, they will spend 840 lira in total, leaving them 160 lira change, which is enough for them to buy an ice cream each as a treat.

PAGE 20

The answer is **C**.

PAGE 21

The answer is a Mediterranean sea turtle.

PAGE 22

PAGE 23

There are 18 marmots.

PAGE 24

The answer is B.

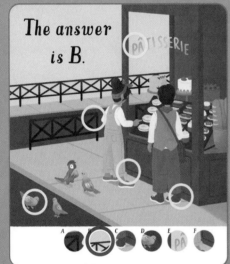

PAGE 26

The answer is Toledo.

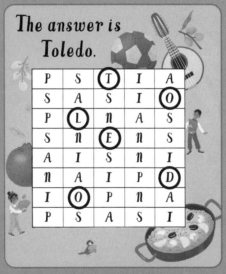

P	S	T	I	A
S	A	S	I	O
P	L	n	A	S
S	n	E	n	S
A	I	S	n	I
n	A	I	P	D
I	O	P	n	A
P	S	A	S	I

PAGE 28

Phoebe will find 19 and Felix will find 18, so Phoebe will find the most.

PAGE 30

The answer is a black rhino.

The answer is C.

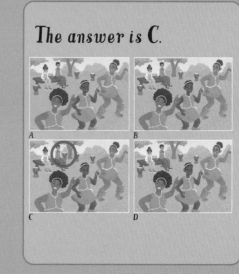

A   B

C   D

The answer is D.

A   B   C   D   E   F

PAGE 37

The answer is
SHIPWRECK.

PAGE 38

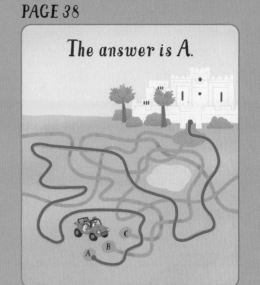

The answer is A.

PAGE 39

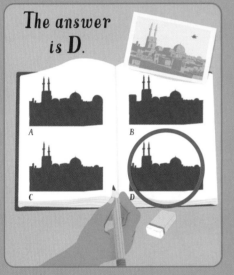

The answer
is D.

PAGE 41

The answer is E.

PAGE 42

The correct order is:

5 8 6 1 9 4 3 2 7 10

PAGE 45

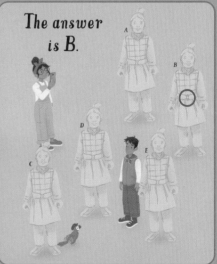

The answer
is B.

The answer is
SHENZHEN.

The answer is C.

The answer is 10.

The answer is
MANILA.

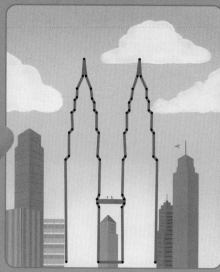

PAGE 53

The answer is C.

PAGE 54

The answer is B.

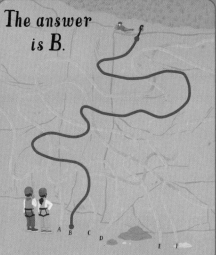

PAGE 55

The answer is WOMBAT.

PAGE 56

PAGE 58

The shell circled in black is the odd one out.

PAGE 60

PAGE 61

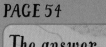

PAGE 62

The answer is C.

PAGE 63

14 squirrels and 15 cacti, so there are more cacti.

PAGE 64

The answer is surfing.

PAGE 66

¢450 + ¢200 + ¢200 + ¢450 + ¢100 = ¢1,400

PAGE 67

The answer is B.

PAGE 68

There are 10 spider monkeys.

PAGE 71

The answer is D.

PAGE 72

PAGE 73

PAGE 74

The answer is E.

PAGE 75

PAGE 76

PAGE 78

The answer is a
giant anteater.

PAGE 79

The answer is C.

PAGE 80

Felix: $5 + $5 + $9 + $2.50 = $21.50

Phoebe: $5 + $7.50 + $6 + $1 = $19.50

Felix pays the most.

PAGE 81

10 bicycles and 9 cabs, so there are more bicycles.

PAGE 82

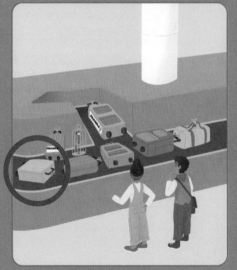

PAGE 84

The answer is E.

PAGE 85